SCHIRMER'S LIBRARY
OF MUSICAL CLASSICS

SALVATORE MARCHESI

Op. 15

Twenty Elementary and Progressive Vocalises

(WITH ITALIAN WORDS)

→ FOR MEDIUM VOICE . . Library Vol. 593
FOR ALTO . . . . Library Vol. 594

English Translations by
GEORGE L. OSGOOD

With a Biographical Sketch of the Author
by
DR. THEODORE BAKER

G. SCHIRMER, Inc.

DISTRIBUTED BY

HAL•LEONARD®
CORPORATION
7777 W. BLUEMOUND RD. P.O. BOX 13819 MILWAUKEE, WI 53213

SALVATORE MARCHESI

SALVATORE MARCHESI (de Castrone), *rectius* Cavaliere Salvatore de Castrone, Marchese della Rajata, the distinguished singing-master, was born on January the 15th, 1822, at Palermo. He comes of noble family; his father was Governor-General of Sicily for four years. At the age of sixteen he joined the aristocratic "Neapolitan Guard," a military organization from which, however, his liberal principles caused him to resign in 1840. Returning to Palermo, he entered upon a course of philosophy and law at the University, at the same time studying singing and composition under Pietro Raimondi. In 1845 he had already attained considerable prominence in musical circles; for, on the establishment of the "Accademia Filarmonica" in his native city, he was appointed delegate for the Musical Association. A year later he went to Milan, where he continued vocal study under Lamperti and Fontana; but by reason of his participation in the revolutionary movement of 1848, he was expelled from Italy, and sought refuge in New York. It was here that he made his début as a baritone in opera (Verdi's *Ernani*). In 1850 the failure of the Italian operatic venture hastened Marchesi's departure from America; he recrossed the ocean, and found a temporary resting-place in London, where he finished his vocal training under Manuel Garcia, and thereafter appeared as a concert-singer under the name of "Marchesi." Successes in London induced him to undertake a concert-tour through Holland and Germany during the winter of 1851–52; he sang in Leipzig, Bremen, Hamburg, Frankfort, and also at the courts of Berlin, Weimar, Hanover, Oldenburg, etc., winning increasing fame and applause. In 1852 he married the celebrated mezzo-soprano Mathilde Graumann, who has since, as "Mathilde Marchesi," become so famous as a singing-teacher. After two years devoted to singing in opera and concert in various capitals (London, Berlin, Brussels, Milan), they were engaged together to instruct the vocal classes at the Vienna Conservatory. Here they remained for seven years (1854–61); then spent three years longer in operatic and concert *tournées*, lived for a time in Paris, and in 1865 were called to the Cologne Conservatory. From 1869 they again taught in the Vienna Conservatory; and since 1881 have been permanently settled in Paris.

Marchesi was appointed "Chamber-singer" to the Grand Duke of Saxe-Weimar in 1862; in recognition of his political activity the King of Italy decorated him with the order of St. Maurice and St. Lazarus.

As a writer, Marchesi has been an active musical correspondent of numerous English, French, German and Italian periodicals. In 1873 he published a book, "Relazione sugli Istrumenti musicali quali erano rappresentati all' Esposizione universale di Vienna nel Giugno," an account of the musical instruments at the Vienna Exposition of that year, at' which he officiated as a juror. He has likewise translated a considerable number of French and German opera-libretti into Italian; notably those of *Iphigénie, Médée, La Vestale, Der fliegende Holländer, Tannhäuser,* and *Lohengrin.*

As a composer he has published a number of settings of French, German and Italian (Neapolitan and Sicilian) songs, distinguished for graceful inspiration. But he is still better known by his "Twenty Elementary and Progressive Vocalises," a "Riassunto dell' arte del canto," and his "Method of Singing," the ripe fruit of a long and brilliant career as a teacher of vocal art. The Vocalises may, in particular, be recommended for developing breadth and suavity of tone, together with clearness and elegance in phrasing.

TH. BAKER.

Twenty Vocalises.

For the Medium of the Voice.

Messa di Voce.

English translations by
George L. Osgood.

SALVATORE C. MARCHESI. Op.15.

Andante mosso.

From ____ God ____ a ____ lone ____ may ____ mor - tals Ask for ____
Al ____ ciel ____ sol ____ può ____ la ____ vi - ta Chie - de -

life and light, ____ No, ____ no ____
re il mor - tal; ____ Non ____ val,

*) Every vocalise is to be sung first on *â* as in father.
The comma (,) denotes inhalation when singing on *â*.
The sign ⊕ denotes inhalation when singing with words.

earth_ly aid or pow___er Can _____ e'er _____
no, ter - re-stre a - i - ta, non _____ val _____

help them love the right._____ From _____
Un po - ter co - tal; _____ Al _____

God _____ a - - lone may _____
ciel _____ sol _____ può _____ la _____

___ mor - tals Ask for life and light._____
___ vi - ta Chie-de - re il mor - tal. _____

Portamento.

hie-ing Re - turns she to flower O'er hill and o'er plain.   Mortals grow old - er,
pri-le, E fresca e gen - ti - le, Ri - tor-n'a fio-rir!   L'uomo s'in - vec-chia

Sadden'd by sor - row, Nor brings the mor - row Their Spring a - gain! Ah why? ah
fra stenti e pe - ne, E mai ri - vie - ne Per lui l'a-pril! Per-chè, per-

why does boun-ti-ful Nature Of each human crea-ture Al - lay not the sorrow? Ah
chè la cal-ma na-tu-ra Le pe-ne non cu-ra Del mi-ser mor-ta-le! Per-

why? ah why? Sweet Nature, re - ply. Ah why? ah why? sweet Nature, re - ply.
chè, per-chè sen-si-bil non è!__ Per-chè, per-chè sen - si-bil non è!

Canto spianato.

3.

Scala diatonica.

Allegro moderato.

I can - not, I — can - not here long-er de - lay _ me, My love does be-
Non pos - so, non pos - so più star-ti lon-ta - no. Il fin-ger è

tray _ me, No long-er _ I'll feign. Then why _ should I _ suf-fer With thought so tor-
va - no, Non va-le il gab-bar. Re - si - ster non vo-glio al cru - do tor-

rall. *a tempo*

ment-ing? A - way _ with la - ment-ing, I _ come, love, a - gain. I can - not, I
men-to. Mo-ri - re mi sen - to, Mi sen - to spi-rar. Non pos - so, non

can-not here long-er de - lay _ me, My love _ does be-tray _ me, No long-er _ I'll feign.
pos - so più star-ti lon-ta - no. Il fin-ger è va - no, Non va-le il gabbar.

Scala diatonica.

find _ no _ re-ward. My moth — er _ com — pels _ me To spin _ and _ to _
tro - vo _ mer-cè. La mam — ma _ mi for - za Mi spin - ge_al la-

la — bor, With care _ for _ a _ neigh - bor, My lot _ is _ too hard. Ah!
vo - ro. Di no - ia _ mi mo - ro, _ Re - si - ster _ non so, no!

Tempo di Valse.　　Scala puntata.

Of _ com - ing _ morn - ing The sky _ gives warn-ing, The_
Già _ sor - ge il gior - no, si le - va il so - le, L'e-

6.

bright _ ho - ri — zon Is her — ald of day. A ros - y _
ter - na _ mo - le Ri - tor - na_a bril-lar. Di ro - seo _

man - tle O'er na - ture is ly - ing, But war - riors are hie - ing In
man - to si cin - ge la ter-ra, Fra gliuo - min' la guer - ra Già

fight - ing ar - ray. A - las!___ with the morning Comes care___ to each one,___When
tor - na a scoppiar. E tor - na col gior-no Nel mon - do il do - lor, si, Col

slumber is o - ver Our peace then has flown! Of___ com - ing morn - ing The
son - no la pa - ce spa - ri - ta è dal cor! Già___ sor - ge il gior - no, Si

sky___ gives warn-ing, The___ bright___ ho - ri - zon Is her - ald of day.
le - va il so - le, L'e - ter - na mo - le Ri - tor - na a bril - lar.

Scala cromatica.

7. Andante.

Rap - id - ly___ time flies a - long Like__ the__ glar - ing__
Vo__ la il__ tem - po__ ra - pi - do, *Al__ par del - la__*

lightning's bend; How__ it___ bears___ with__ might - y power
fol - go - re, *E___ co - m'es - sa in - do - mi - to*

Man - kind__ to___ their__ end! To___ our hopes and to our love,
Strug - ge il__ mon - do o - gnor. *La___ spe - ran - za, l'i - do - lo*

To___ what - e'er the heart may move, Time__ the___ mas - ter
Del - la schiat - tau - ma - na, *Tal__ ti - ran - no*

Scala minore.

me Heav-y - heart - ed. Of all the fair - est, Woman the rar - est,
pe-so la vi - ta Don-na co-tan - ta Madre si ra - ra,

Tempo I.

There is no oth - er Like to my mother. An gels___ in bright ar -
Nes-sun' al mon-do tro-var la può.___ La___ ca - ra ma - dre

ray___ Bore___ my___ sweet mother a - way! O saint - ed___
mi - a, Mo - ri - a, E___ più non è! A - ma - ta___

moth - er, Now tru - ly blessed, A - mong___ the ho - ly Thou art___ at rest! ah!
tan - to Da tut - ti___ fù, Spa - ri___ d'in - can - to, Ahi! non___ è più, ah!

Note ripetute.

love a ____ lone Bring - eth __ joy __ to __ ev - 'ry
mor, l'a - - mor Il __ sol __ be - ne __ da - to al

rall.

a tempo

one. Not a joy ____ a __ heart know - eth Till an -
cor. Non ha gio - ia __ il __ co - re Tran - ne il

oth - er - be - stow - eth All its ad - o -
ve - ro - a - mo - re, E l'af - fet - to ____

ra - tion And its con - so - la - tion.
so - lo __ È l'u - man ____ con - so - lo.

Allegro.   Terzine.

Po - ems de - vis - ing, Songs im-pro - vis - ing, Danc-ing and
Mi sen-to un'e - stro D'im-prov-vi - sa - re, Vor - rei can-

sing - ing, Through life I go; Nev - er a sor - row
ta - re, Vor - rei bal - lar. Ho tut - ta l'a - ni - ma

Or care I bor - row, Life is an ec - sta - sy, All joy, no
Di gio - ja pie - na, Mi sen-to in e - sta - si qua - si nel

Tempo I.

woe. Sing we and dance, and dance, Mer - ry be the glance,
Ciel! Can - tiam, bal - liam, bal - liam Ca - ria - mi - cian - diam,

Quartine.

glo - - ry For - sak - ing__ her he ma - ted. My moth - er__ once__ to__
gli uo - mi - ni, Ah! sem - pre co - sì sa - rà. La ma - dre mia__ di -

me__ did say That in____ the____ old - en____ by - gone day The
ce - va - mi, Che in tem - pi più__ pro - pi - zi - i Non

world was__ bet - ter__ then, than now, That men__ were true__ and kept their vow.
v'e - ran tan - ti__ vi - zi - i, E il mon - do e - ra__ mi - glior.__

world was__ bet - ter__ then, than now, That men__ were true__ and kept their vow.
v'e - ran tan - ti__ vi - zi - i, E il mon - do e - ra__ mi - glior.

Arpeggio

la — bor re — pay — ing, With free — dom from care. It nev — er a-
pi — ta è o-gni bra — ma, La pa — ce tor — na. Non gio — va non

vails — us When ran — cor as — sails — us, For life is but a day,— And —
va — le Di dar — si uel ma — le È un gior — no la vi — ta, la —

stentate **Tempo I.**

night — is soon here. The trum — pets' — warn-ing, The trum — pets —
not — te è già là. La trom — ba — squil-la, la trom — ba —

colla parte

cresc.

warn-ing, Re — minds — us — of — morn — ing, 'Tis time — now for rest.
squil-la, La fiam — ma — scin-til — la, a let — to o-ra an-diam.

cresc.

f

Appoggiatura ed Acciaccatura.

Andante espressivo.

Have mer - cy, Lord, on me—Thy child, Be - hold my
Pie - tà, mio Dio, d'un mi - se - ro, D'un tri - ste af-

con - trite heart,_____ For Thou art mer - ci - ful and mild, My
fran - to cor,_____ Che in te sol spe - ra bal - sa - mo, Soc-

più mosso

hope my all,_ my all Thou art. In - cline Thine ear my prayer to
cor - so al suo,_ al suo do - lor. Dal ciel mi vol - gi il guardo oh! si -

hear. Oh help me my sor - row and an - guish to bear, That death may
gnor. Ri - mi - ra l'an - go - scia, l'e - stre - mo do - lor, Con - ce - di al-

Mordente e Gruppetto.

Allegretto grazioso.

14.

Dear maidens all, if you be-lieve The prophe - cy I
Don - net-te mie, se cre-de-re Po - te-te all'in-do -

make you, Then hasten, pray, the truth receive, And val - iant husbands
vi - no, Non v'è gran tempo a per-de-re, Cer - ca-te ma-ri -

take—you. Now lay a-side your flirting way, Be mod - est and re -
ti - no. Non fa-te tan-te smor-fi - e, Deh! sia-te più mo -

tir - ing, Lest you should miss that wed-ding-day Your hearts are all de -
de - ste, Se no, po - trà suc-ce-der-vi Che tar-di al fin sa -

siring. By doz-ens husbands are for sale, Of ev-'ry age and
rà. Ve n'è doz-zi-ne a ven-de-re, Di tut-te le sta-

sta-tion, Both large and small, or dark or pale, Of al-most ev-'ry_
gio-ni, Ve n'è dei grandi e pic-co-li, E d'o-gni qua-li-

slargando

colla parte

a tempo

na-tion. Then maidens all, of ev-'ry clime, I pray you, do not
tà. Sbri - ga-te-vi, sbri - ga-te-vi, Men-tre pur tempo an-

a tempo

tar - ry; Be-think you now while there is time, If e'er you choose to__
co - ra. Pen - sa-te-vi, pen - sa-te-vi, che il tem-po ve la__

Tempo I.

marry. Dear maidens all, if you be-lieve The proph-e - cy I
fa. Don - net-te mie, se cre-de - re Vo - le - te all'in-do-

make you, Then hasten, pray, the truth re-ceive, And va - liant husbands
vi - no, Non v'è gran tem-po_a per-de - re, Cer-ca - te ma-ri-

rall. *a tempo*

take__you. Now lay a-side your flirt-ing way, Be mod-est and re-
ti - no. Non fa-te tan - te smor-fi - e, Deh! sia - te più mo-

rall. *a tempo*

tir - ing, Lest you should miss that wedding-day Your hearts are all de - siring.
de - ste, Se no po - trà suc - ce-der-vi, Che tar-di_al fin sa - rà.

colla voce

Sincope.

Salti.

Allegretto.

Palpi‑tate, palpi‑tate, Beat at thy pleas‑ure, Ne'er to thy measure, O heart, will I
Palpi‑ta, palpi‑ta, tan‑to che vuo‑i, Ai mo‑ti tuo‑i Non ce‑do, mio

yield me. Pal‑pi‑tate, pal‑pi‑tate, Beat at thy pleas‑ure, Ne'er to thy meas‑ure, O
co‑re. Pal‑pi‑ta, pal‑pi‑ta, tan‑to che vuo‑i, Ai mo‑ti tuo‑i no,

heart, will I yield. Vain‑ly con‑fus‑ing me, Vain‑ly a‑mus‑ing me, Thou art too
Non ce‑de‑rò. In‑dar‑no stuz‑zi‑chi, In‑va‑no piz‑zi‑chi, Non ce‑do,

fan‑ci‑ful, I most un‑mer‑ci‑ful, Courage shall fail me not, no, nev‑er‑more.
cre‑di‑lo, Re‑si‑sto, ve‑di‑lo. Non voglio ar‑ren‑der‑mi al tuo vo‑ler.

colla parte

Tempo I.

Pal-pi-tate, pal-pi-tate, Beat at thy pleasure, Ne'er to thy measure O heart, will I yield me.
Pal-pi - ta, pal-pi-ta, tan-to che vuo-i, Ai mo-ti tuo-i Non ce-do, mio co-re.

Pal-pi-tate, pal-pi-tate, Beat at thy pleasure, Ne'er to thy measure, O heart, will I yield.
Pal-pi - ta, pal-pi-ta, non ce-de - rò, no! Pal-pi-ta, palpi-ta, non ce-de - rò.

Marcato e staccato.

Andante.

What with all this toil and bother, Working ev - er night and day, Know I
Non so più co - sa mi fac-cia, Notte e gior-no a la-vo-rar, Chi mi

17.

well, some day or other It will wear my life__ a - way. Do I well or do I bad-ly, Just the
sgri - da, chi mi-naccia, Son vi - ci-no da__cre-par. Se fo ma-le, se fo be-ne, Ab lo

Trillo.

Andante espressivo.

18.

Tell me why, with glance so frown - ing, Thou re-gard-est me, my
Perchè -mai co - sì tur - ba - ta Tu mi guardi, oh! mio te -

treas - ure! For I love thee with - out meas - ure, And I
so - ro? Tu sai ben, quan-to t'a - do - ro, E che

live a - lone for thee. Ah! the love thou art dis -
vi - vo sol per te. Questo a - mo - re, che m'in -

own - ing Is so pure and faith - ful
fiam - ma, È sì pu - ro ed in no -

Résumé I.

Andantino mosso.

19.

A_zure-like shad_ows Fall on the o_cean, While in the meadows The
Bella è _ l'az_zur_ra, lie_ta ma_ri_na, Ma la col_li_na Co-

blos_soms are fair.— Fair is the o_cean, Endless and grand its mo_tion,
per_ taè di fior.— Son bel_le l'on_de, Del mar, del mar le_spon_de,

But woods and mead_ows, They, too, are fair,— are_ fair, are_ fair.
Ma gliantriei bo_schi Son_ bel_lian_cor,— an_cor, an_cor.

Ah! surely Na_ture has beauty ev'_rywhere, ev'_ry where!— ah! sure_ly
Ah! la na_tu_ra è grande, sì è grande, grande_o_gnor!— ah! sì, la_ na-

where, _____ Ah! _ sure-ly Na - - - - ture_ has beauty ev -'ry- where.
gnor, _____ Ah! sì, la_ na-tu - - - ra _ è_ grande, grande o -gnor!_

Résumé II.

Allegro vivace.

20.

As riv- ers speeding, Their course un - heeding, Go wind - ing_
*I - gna - ro il ri - o del suo de - sti - no, Ser - pen - do_*

on - ward_ Al - way_ sea-ward, Run mur - m'ring for-ward, And ev - er_
cor - re al ma - re in se - no, E mor - mo - ran-do va nel cam -

down-ward To find at last, to find at last On o-cean's breast a home; So
mi - no, Fin-chè al mar, fin-chè al mar si fonde e ta-ce al-lor. Co -